Andrew Brodie Basics

LET'S DO HANDWRITING

FOR AGES 8-9

with over **100** reward stickers

- Structured practice of handwriting strokes
- Extra tips on style and tidiness
- Regular progress checks

Published 2014 by Bloomsbury Publishing Plc
50 Bedford Square, London, WC1B 3DP

www.bloomsbury.com

Bloomsbury is a registered trade mark of Bloomsbury Publishing Plc

ISBN 978-14729-1026-4

First published 2014
© 2014 Andrew Brodie
Cover and inside illustrations of Martha the Meerkat and Andrew Brodie © 2014 Nikalas Catlow
Other inside illustrations © 2014 Steve Evans

A CIP catalogue for this book is available from the British Library.

1 0 9 8 7 6 5 4 3 2

Printed in China by Leo Paper Products

This book is produced using paper that is made from wood grown in managed, sustainable forests. It is natural, renewable and recyclable. The logging and manufacturing process conform to the environmental regulations of the country of origin.

To see our full range of titles visit **www.bloomsbury.com**

BLOOMSBURY

Notes for parents

What's in this book

This is the fourth in the series of *Andrew Brodie Basics Let's Do Handwriting* books. Each book features a clearly structured approach to developing and improving children's handwriting, an essential skill for correct spelling and effective written communication. Check the handwriting style used at your child's school as there are slight variations between schools. The style used in this book reflects the most popular one.

The National Curriculum states that, during early Key Stage 2, children should use the diagonal and horizontal strokes needed to join letters but they recognise that some letters should remain unjoined at this stage. They increase the legibility, consistency and quality of their handwriting: they attempt to keep downstrokes of letters parallel and equidistant and they ensure that lines of writing are spaced so that the ascenders and descenders of letters do not collide. Enjoying the practice in this book will help your child to achieve all of these skills.

How you can help

Make sure your child is ready for their handwriting practice. They should be able to place this book flat on a desk or table; make sure that their chair and table are of appropriate heights so that they are comfortable and can reach their work easily. Check that the work area is well-lit with clear, uncluttered space.

Your child should hold the book at an appropriate angle so that their handwriting is clearly visible to them. If your child is left-handed, the book will need to be turned to the opposite angle to that used by right-handed people: it is essential that they can see their work, rather than covering it with their hand as they write.

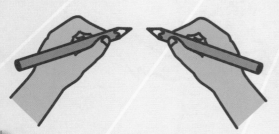

Martha the Meerkat

Look out for Martha the Meerkat, who tells your child what to focus on ready for the progress check at the end of each section.

Andrew Brodie says…

On some pages there are further tips and reminders from Andrew Brodie, which are devised to encourage your child to self-check their work.

When your child does well, makes sure you tell them so! The colourful stickers in the middle of this book can be a great reward for good work and a big incentive for future progress.

The answer section

The answer section at the back of this book can be a useful teaching tool: ask your child to compare their handwriting to the exemplars shown on the progress check 'answers'. If they have written their letters and words correctly, congratulate them, but if they haven't, don't let them worry about it! Instead, encourage them to learn the correct versions. Give lots of praise for any success.

Practise letters c, o, a and d

One of the letters on this page has an ascender. Ascend means to go up. Can you guess which letter?

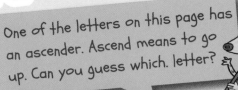

Practise writing the letter c.

Try writing c again but this time smaller.

Practise writing the letter o.

Now try a smaller version.

Practise writing the letter a.

Now try a smaller version.

Practise writing the letter d.

Now try a smaller version.

Lots of letters can be joined using a slope join.

Practise writing the words.   addd

add addd add add addd

Try writing add again but this time smaller.

add addd add add dddd add addd addd add

do do do do do do do

Try writing do again but this time smaller.

do do do do do do do do do do do do do do do do do

dad dad dad dad

Try writing dad again but this time smaller.

dad dad dodd dod dad dad dad ddd dad dad

cad cad cad

Try writing cad again but this time smaller.

cad cad cad cad cad cad cad cad cad cad cad cad

Well Done

Andrew Brodie says...
Make sure that the letter **d** is taller than the other letters.
Make sure that the letters **c**, **o** and **a** are all the same size.

22/07/24

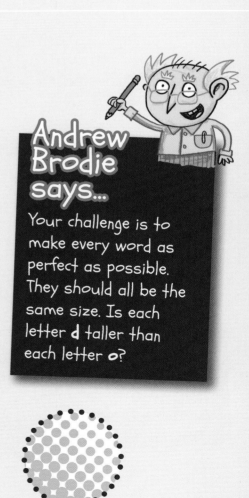

Letter **o** joins to **n** with a bridge join

First, practise writing the letter n.

 n n n n

Try writing n again but this time smaller.

n n n n

When joining from a letter o we use a bridge join instead of a slope join.

 on on on on

Try writing on again but this time smaller.

on on on on

How many times can you write the word dodo around the picture?

dodo

Andrew Brodie says...

Your challenge is to make every word as perfect as possible. They should all be the same size. Is each letter **d** taller than each letter **o**?

Practise writing the letter e.

Try writing e again but this time smaller.

e   e   e   e

Look at this letter e, which is used when we make a slope join from another letter.

 e   e   e

Try writing e again but this time smaller.

e   e   e   e

Practise these words, which use the sloping letter e.

code   code   code
cane   cane   cane
done   done   done

Andrew Brodie says...
Remember to use a bridge join from each letter **o**. Make sure that the letter **d** is taller than the other letters and that the **c**, **o** and **a** are all the same size.

Practise n, m and h

Letters **m** and **h** are quite similar to a letter **n**.

Practise writing the letter n again.

 n n n n n n

Now try a smaller letter n.

n n n n

Practise writing the letter m.

 m m m m

Now try writing m again but this time smaller.

m m m m

Practise writing the letter h.

 h h h h

Try writing h again but this time smaller.

h h h h

Practise writing these words, which use the sloping letter e.

home home home
name name name
made made made

7

Write each letter 15 times.
Try to keep them all the same size.

a

c

o

d

e

n

h

m

Write the word home as many times as you can inside the house.

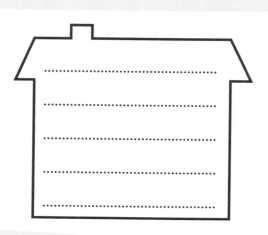

Andrew Brodie says...

Don't forget to use bridge joins from each letter o.

Write each word five times.

hand

mend

made

mood

Write the word moon all round the picture. You will need to turn the book around as you write.

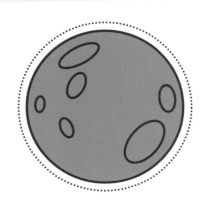

Practise letters g, y and j

Letters **g y** and **j** have descenders which descend through the writing line.

Practise writing the letter g.

Try writing g again but this time smaller.

g g g g

Practise writing the letter y.

Now try a smaller version.

y y y y

Practise writing the letter j.

Now try a smaller version.

 j j j

Practise writing these words. Notice that we are not joining from the letters that have descenders.

jade jade jade
dog dog dog
day day day
jam jam jam
good good good

9

Practise letters b and p

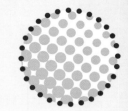

Practise writing the letter b.

b b b b

Practise writing the letter p.

p p p p

Now try these words. Notice that we are not joining from b or p.

boom boom boom
abode abode abode
pond pond pond
band band band
pony pony pony
cab cab cab
cap cap cap
baboon baboon baboon
panda panda panda
poem poem poem
mop mop mop
map map map

Letters **b** and **p** are formed in similar ways but one has an ascender and one has a descender.

Andrew Brodie says...

Make sure that the letter **b** is taller than the other letters and that letter **p** goes through the writing line. Are the round part of your letter **b** and the round part of your letter **p** exactly the same size as the other letters?

Letters i, l and k

Did you know that you have to go back to put a dot over the letter i after you have finished the word?

Practise writing the letter i.

i i i i i

Practise writing the letter l.

l l l l l

Practise writing the letter k.

k k k k k

Now try these words.

milk milk milk
lick lick lick
kick kick kick
pick pick pick
pink pink pink
bank bank bank
ball ball ball
blink blink blink

Andrew Brodie says...

Try to make every copy of each word look exactly the same and remember not to join from the letters **b** or **p**.

Letter **s** starts like a letter **c** but wiggles round!

Practise writing the letter s.

s s s s

Look at letter r – it is quite like letter n. Practise writing the letters r and n.

r r r r

n n n n

Practise the bridge join from letter r.

ro ro ro

ri ri ri

re re re

ra ra ra

Now try these words. Notice that we are not joining from letter s.

soon soon soon

spoon spoon spoon

spins spins spins

rinse rinse rinse

drain drain drain

harp harp harp

sharp sharp sharp

shape shape shape

Andrew Brodie says...

Make sure that the letter **s** and the letter **r** are the same size as the letter **o**. Remember to use a bridge join from the letter **r**.

Practise letters t and f

Letter t is a bit like a letter l but it is not as tall.

Practise writing the letter t.

t · · t · · t · · t

Look at letter f – it is quite tall and it has a descender.

f · f · f · f

Practise the bridge join from letter f.

fo   fo   fo
fi   fi   fi
fa   fa   fa
fe   fe   fe

Now try these words.

tired   tired   tired
fitted   fitted   fitted
fright   fright   fright
often   often   often
office   office   office

Andrew Brodie says...

Don't forget to go back to dot the letter i and to cross the letter t after you have finished the word.

Write each letter 15 times.
Try to keep them all the same size.

t
f
r
s
i
l
k
b
p

Write the word
milk as many
times as you
can inside the
bottle.

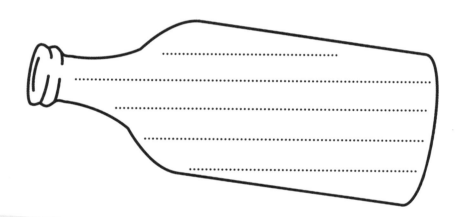

Write each word five times.

spinner
trainers
shorts
pocket

Write the word
train inside each
carriage.

14

Practise letters u, v and w

Letter **w** is more like a double **v** than a double **u**!

Practise writing the letter v.

v   v   v   v

Try writing v again but this time smaller.

v   v   v   v

Practise writing the letter w.

w   w   w   w

Try writing w again but this time smaller.

w   w   w   w

Practise writing the letter u.

u   u   u   u

Try writing u again but this time smaller.

u   u   u   u

Practise writing these words.

west west west
western western western
westerly westerly westerly
vest vest vest
invest invest invest
under under under
underneath underneath underneath

15

Practise writing the letter q. It is has a descender.

q   q   q   q

Try writing q again but this time smaller.

q   q   q   q

Practise writing q and u together. You can join the q to the u if you want to, by using a slope join.

qu   qu   qu   qu

Write these words as neatly as you can.

quite quite quite

quiet quiet quiet

quad quad quad

quip quip quip

equip equip equip

equipment equipment equipment

require require require

requirement requirement requirement

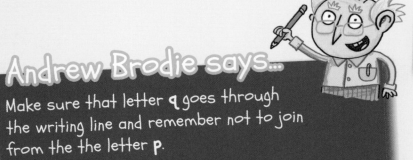

Andrew Brodie says...

Make sure that letter **q** goes through the writing line and remember not to join from the the letter **p**.

Letter **q** is always followed by letter **u**.

Letters x and z

Practise writing the letter x.

  X   X   X

Practise writing the letter z.

  Z   Z   Z

Practise writing both letters together but do not join them.

xz xz xz

zx zx zx

We can join to the letter x or to the letter z from other letters but we don't join from them.

Now try these words.

excuse excuse excuse

mixture mixture mixture

fixed fixed fixed

lazy lazy lazy

laziness laziness laziness

hazy hazy hazy

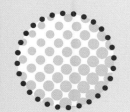

Andrew Brodie says...

Try to make every copy of each word look the same and remember not to join from **x** or **z**.

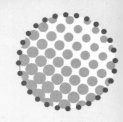

Practise writing the capital letters.

A A A A

B B B B

C C C C

D D D D

E E E E

F F F F

G G G G

H H H H

I I I I

J J J J

K K K K

L L L L

M M M M

Practise capital letters

Practise writing the capital letters.

Capital letters are used at the starts of sentences, names, days and months.

N N N N
O O O O
P P P P
Q Q Q Q
R R R R
S S S S
T T T T
U U U U
V V V V
W W W W
X X X X
Y Y Y Y
Z Z Z Z

Write each letter 15 times.
Try to keep them all the same size.

A

q

y

x

Q

z

F

w

R

u

Write the word quilt as many times as you can on the bed quilt.

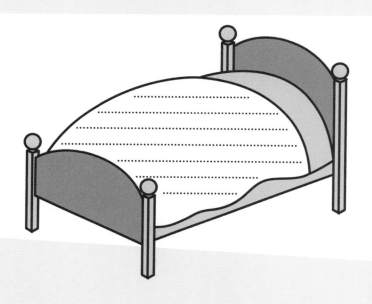

Write each word five times.

request

xylophone

zoology

waterside

rewind

Practise double letter o

Practise writing double o.

Practise writing these oo words.

room room room
broom broom broom
soon soon soon
sooner sooner sooner
bloom bloom bloom
spoon spoon spoon
zookeeper zookeeper zookeeper
fool fool fool
foolish foolish foolish
foolishly foolishly foolishly

Sometimes we can use writing within a picture or poem and we don't always join the letters. Try writing zoom like this:

zoom

Andrew Brodie says...

Remember not to join from **b**, **p**, **z** or **s**. Use a bridge join from a letter **r** or letter **o**.

Practise double letter r

Letter **r** joins to another letter **r** with a bridge join.

Practise writing double r.

 rr

Practise writing these rr words.

arrange arrange arrange
arranging arranging arranging
arrangement arrangement arrangement
horror horror horror
horrible horrible horrible
horrific horrific horrific
horrify horrify horrify
horrified horrified horrified
carrier carrier carrier
borrowing borrowing borrowing

Sometimes we can use writing within a picture and we don't always join the letters. Try writing Grr like this:

Andrew Brodie says...

Remember not to join from **g** or **b**. Use a bridge join from a letter **r** or letter **o**.

Make sure that letters with ascenders are tall and that letters with descenders go through the line.

Practise double letter s

We are not joining letter **s** to letters that follow it.

Practise writing double s. Make sure every letter s is the same size as a letter o.

boss

Practise writing these ss words.

boss boss boss
bossy bossy bossy
bossiness bossiness bossiness
class class class
grass grass grass
pass pass pass
passed passed passed
miss miss miss
missing missing missing
missed missed missed

Sometimes we can use writing within a picture and we don't always join the letters. Try writing hiss like this:

hisssss

Andrew Brodie says...
Remember not to join from **s**, **g** or **b**.

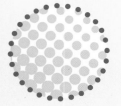

Practise double letter l

We use a slope join to join a letter l to another letter l.

Practise writing all. Make sure every letter l is taller than letter a.

all all all

Practise writing these ll words.

falling falling falling
fell fell fell
call call call
calling calling calling
called called called
allow allow allow
allowing allowing allowing
allowed allowed allowed
bellow bellow bellow
bellowed bellowed bellowed

Sometimes we can use writing within a picture and we don't always join the letters. Try writing fall like this:

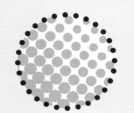

Andrew Brodie says...

Remember to join from the cross on the **f**. Make sure that letters with ascenders are tall and that letters with descenders go through the line.

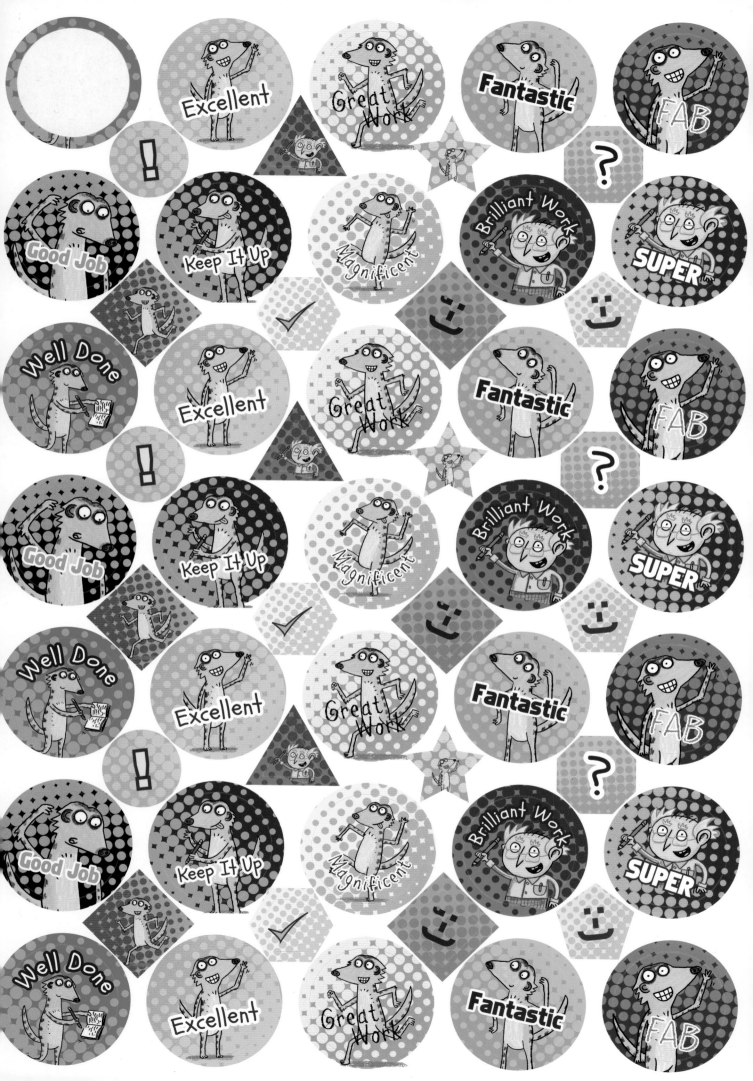

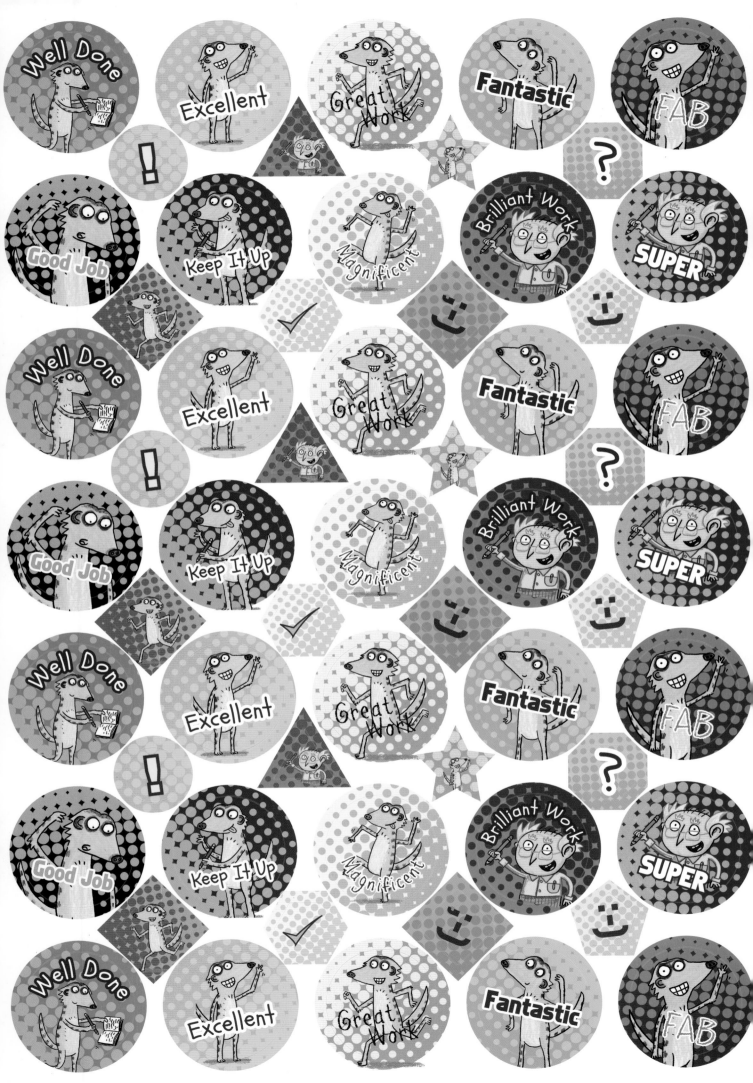

Practise double letter t

Practise writing double t.
You can cross both letters with one line.

tt   tt   tt   tt

Practise writing these tt words.

batting batting batting
butter butter butter
buttering buttering buttering
buttered buttered buttered
kettle kettle kettle
nettle nettle nettle
knitting knitting knitting
attitude attitude attitude
letter letter letter
lettering lettering lettering

Practise this short sentence.

Is butter better?

Andrew Brodie says...
Remember to go back to cross each letter
t. You can use one line to cross both letters
at the same time.

Write each word or pair of letters eight times.
Try to keep them all the same size.

ll

wall

oo

room

ss

pass

tt

dotty

rr

starry

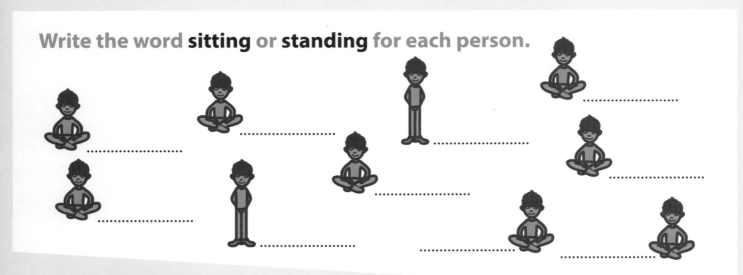

Write the word sitting or standing for each person.

Write each word three times.

arrangement

carefully

missing

fluttering

flooring

Practise question marks

Every question needs a question mark.

Practise writing a question mark.

? ? ? ?

Match the questions to the answers. Write each question followed by the appropriate answer.

Cardiff

Edinburgh

What is the capital city of England?

What is the capital city of Wales?

What is the capital city of Northern Ireland?

What is the capital city of Scotland?

Belfast

London

Andrew Brodie says...

Remember that a question mark is the same height as a tall letter. Don't forget to use capital letters for place names and for the start of each sentence.

Questions to answer

Use your very best handwriting on this page.

Write your own answers to these questions. Try to use full sentences to answer the questions and give as much information as you can.

What is your name?

How old are you?

When is your birthday?

What school do you go to?

Who is your best friend?

What is your favourite colour?

Do you have a hobby?

Andrew Brodie says...

Now go back over your work and see if there is anything you can improve on.

Speech marks

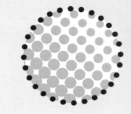

Speech marks are short lines that curve slightly.

"When is your birthday?" asked Tariq.
"On the twenty-sixth of January," replied Andy.

Speech marks are written at the start and at the end of words that somebody speaks.

Andrew Brodie says...

Did you notice that the question mark and the comma both appeared before the closing set of speech marks?

Now try copying out this conversation. Notice that a new line is started each time the speaker changes.

"Have you seen my new bike?" said Tom proudly.
"Yes, what about it?" asked Sam.
"Nice, isn't it?"
"It's all right," commented Sam.
"Don't you like it?" asked Tom.
"Of course I do, it's great!" exclaimed Sam.

Another conversation

I like talking! Can you write down what might be said in this interview?

Imagine that you are being interviewed on the television. The interviewer is asking you questions about a special day. Write your own answers to the questions.

"Have you had a good day today?" asked the reporter.

"What was the best part about your day?" she asked.

"Was there anything you didn't like about today?" she continued.

"Do you think tomorrow is going to be a good day?" she asked.

"Is there anything you would like to add?" she said.

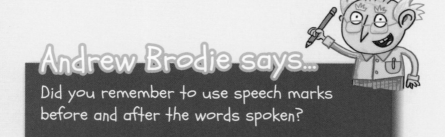

Andrew Brodie says...
Did you remember to use speech marks before and after the words spoken?

Write your own conversation

My birthday is in June. I love having my party in the summer.

next   November   April   last   June

May   January   March   February   July   September

birthday   present   party   invitation   October   December   August

Write a conversation that you could have with a friend about your birthday. The words above may give you some ideas.

Andrew Brodie says...

Did you remember to use speech marks before and after the words spoken and to start a new line when the speaker changed?

31

Copy the question mark as neatly as you can, 15 times. Try to keep them all the same size.

? ? ?

Write each sentence carefully:

"Hello," said Tim.
"Goodbye," said Emily.

"How are you?" asked Mr Patel.
"Very well, thank you," said Mrs Smith.

"Do you know where my book is?"
asked Jasdeep.
"Where you left it, I expect," replied Kelda.

Writing rhymes

Use your best handwriting to copy the rhymes on this page.

I wish that I could find the time,
To write with words that scan and rhyme.

I'd write in such attractive verse,
That I could learn and then rehearse.

I'd stand up proudly on the stage,
And say my verse to every age.

And they would clap and they would cheer,
Oh, why can't I defeat my fear?

We usually start each line of a rhyme with a capital letter.

Haiku

Haiku are very short poems.

Use your best handwriting to copy the haiku poems on this page. Most haiku poems have three lines. They often have five syllables in the first line, seven in the second line and five in the third.

The woods are on fire.
Forceful fearsome forest flames
Forever frighten.

Summer is coming.
Swallows flying from the south.
Leaves bursting with green.

My dog doesn't bark.
He miaows like a tom cat.
I like him like that.

Miaow!

Andrew Brodie says...
Don't forget to use your best handwriting.

34

Acrostic poems

Copying poems is a great way to practise handwriting.

Use your best handwriting to copy the acrostic poem. Acrostics are written so that the first letters of each line spell out a word. You could make the first letter stand out by writing it extra large.

Summer is the best time.
Under the shade of trees we can sit.
My holidays will be great.
My friends will come round.
Every day we can play.
Rolling and cycling and running.

Now try writing your own acrostic poem. Perhaps you could write one about winter.

Cinquain poems

Cinquain is pronounced sin cane. Some words sound different to how they look.

Cinquain poems have five lines and a special syllable pattern. Copy out the syllable pattern.

Two syllables.
Four syllables.
Six syllables.
Eight syllables.
Two syllables.

Use you best handwriting to copy this cinquain poem. Notice that it is written in a diamond pattern.

My dog
Likes the old cat.
But the new cat is fierce
So the dog runs away to hide.
Poor dog.

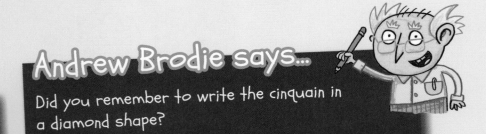

Andrew Brodie says...

Did you remember to write the cinquain in a diamond shape?

Limericks

Limericks are usually quite funny.

Limericks have five lines and a special rhythm.

Use your best handwriting to copy this limerick.

There was a young lady called Bella
Who couldn't close up her umbrella.
The wind blew quite hard
Right through the back yard,
And the brolly became a propellor!

Now try this one.

There was a young teacher called Tony
Who rode into school on a pony.
"You can't bring that here!"
The kids said with a cheer.
So he gave them a stare, which was stony.

Andrew Brodie says...

Can you see the rhyming pattern in each limerick?
Did you write them in your best handwriting?

Write the alphabet in capitals on the wavy line.

A B C D E F G H I J K L M N O P Q R S T U V W X Y Z

Write the alphabet in lower case letters on the wavy line. Look carefully at which letters join to the letters following them.

abcdefghijklmnopqrstuvwxyz

Copy the rhyme and then the cinquain poem really neatly.

This is the way
To do writing today.

My house
Is quite little.
There are two rooms downstairs,
Up the stairs there are just two more.
It's home.

Short story

Finished stories must be written in your best handwriting.

Copy the story carefully. You can write some extra at the end if you want to.

I flew higher into the sky and soon I was able to look down on my own home. It looked so different from above. I could see the outline of the house and the garage. I could see the pathway winding to the front door. What worried me, though, was that someone was walking up that path.

How good is your pencil control? Can you copy this triangle really carefully? You will need to use a ruler.

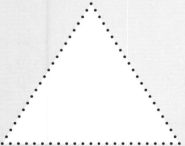

Andrew Brodie says...

Make sure your triangle is as neat as possible.

Conversation

Copy the conversation carefully. You can write some extra at the end if you want to.

"What are you doing here?" the teacher asked.
"I came to see you," I replied.
"Oh good. How can I help you?" she said.
"I'd like to go on the school trip, please,"
I smiled.
"That's great news!" she exclaimed.

How good is your pencil control? Can you copy this square really carefully? You will need to use a ruler.

Andrew Brodie says...
Make sure your square is as neat as possible.

40

Argument

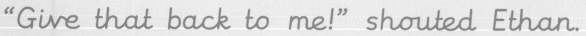

Exclamation marks are used when somebody says something strongly.

Copy the conversation carefully.
You can write some extra at the end if you want to.

"Give that back to me!" shouted Ethan.
"No, it's mine!" said Fern crossly.
"It definitely is not!" replied Ethan.
"It certainly is! I had it for my birthday."
"Who gave it to you then?" asked Ethan.
"You did!" she exclaimed triumphantly.

How good is your pencil control? Can you copy this
rectangle really carefully? You may need to use a ruler.

Play script

I like appearing in plays. I'm a star!

Copy the start of this play script about a girl who has forgotten to do her homework. You can write some extra at the end if you want to. Notice that there are no speech marks in play scripts.

Teacher: Could you all pass me your homework sheets, please.

Alice: I forgot to do it. What am I going to do?

Ben: You are going to be in trouble.

Alice: Can't you help me?

Ben: What am I supposed to do to help?

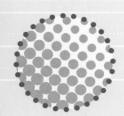

How good is your pencil control? Can you copy this star really carefully? You will need to use a ruler.

Andrew Brodie says...

Make sure your star is as neat as possible.

Handwriting tips

By now you should know lots of tips for good handwriting.

Copy out the tips in your very best handwriting.

Capital letters and letters with ascenders should be taller than most letters.

Most letters should sit neatly on the writing line.

Letters with descenders should pass through the writing line.

Most letters should join to the letters that follow them.

Punctuation marks should be written in the right places.

Neat handwriting looks really good and is much easier for people to read.

Copy this conversation very neatly.

"What is the capital city of Australia?"
asked the teacher.
"I think it's Canberra," the pupil replied.

Use your best handwriting to copy the start of this short story.

Just as the clock struck midnight, Sam
sat up in bed. Now was his chance! He
slipped out of bed as quietly as he could
then tiptoed over to the door. The hinges
squeaked slightly as Sam pulled the door
open, but nobody else seemed to hear them.

ANSWERS

Talk about the progress checks with your child, encouraging him/her to match each one with the copies shown here.

Andrew Brodie says...

Check the following:

- Are the letters consistent in size?
- Does your child remember to make the letters taller with descenders than the other letters?
- Do the letters sit neatly on the writing lines?
- Do the letters with descenders such as g, p and y go through the line?
- Is letter j written correctly? Does it go through the line? Has it got a dot, like a letter i?
- Are most of the letters joined?
- Does your child remember not to join from letters b, g, j, p, q, s, x and z?

Progress Check 1

Write each letter 15 times.
Try to keep them all the same size.

a   a a a a a a a a a a a a a a a
c   c c c c c c c c c c c c c c
o   o o o o o o o o o o o o o o o
d   d d d d d d d d d d d d d
e   e e e e e e e e e e e e e e
n   n n n n n n n n n n n n n n
h   h h h h h h h h h h h h h h
m   m m m m m m m m m m m m m m m

Write the word **home** as many times as you can inside the house.

home home
home home
home home
home home
home home

Andrew Brodie says...

Don't forget to use bridge joins from each letter o

Write each word five times.

hand   hand hand hand hand hand
mend   mend mend mend mend mend
made   made made made made made
mood   mood mood mood mood mood

Write the word **moon** all round the picture. You will need to turn the book around as you write.

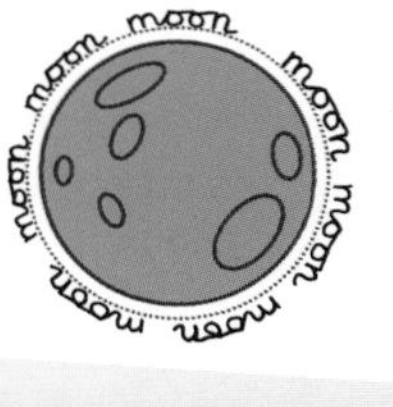

8

45

Write each letter 15 times.
Try to keep them all the same size.

t t t t t t t t t t t t t t t t
f f f f f f f f f f f f f f f f
r r r r r r r r r r r r r r r
s s s s s s s s s s s s s s s s
i i i i i i i i i i i i i i i i
l l l l l l l l l l l l l l l
k k k k k k k k k k k k k k
b b b b b b b b b b b b b b b
P P P P P P P P P P P P P P P

Write the word **milk** as many times as you can inside the bottle.

Write each word five times.

spinner spinner spinner spinner spinner spinner
trainers trainers trainers trainers trainers trainers
shorts shorts shorts shorts shorts shorts
pocket pocket pocket pocket pocket pocket

Write the word **train** inside each carriage.

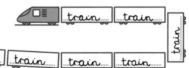

14

Write each letter 15 times.
Try to keep them all the same size.

A A A A A A A A A A A A A A
q q q q q q q q q q q q q q q
Y Y Y Y Y Y Y Y Y Y Y Y Y Y
x x x x x x x x x x x x x x x
Q Q Q Q Q Q Q Q Q Q Q Q Q Q
z z z z z z z z z z z z z z z
F F F F F F F F F F F F F F F
w w w w w w w w w w w w w w w
R R R R R R R R R R R R R R R
u u u u u u u u u u u u u u u u

Write the word **quilt** as many times as you can on the bed quilt.

Write each word five times.

request request request request request request
xylophone xylophone xylophone xylophone xylophone
zoology zoology zoology zoology zoology zoology
waterside waterside waterside waterside waterside
rewind rewind rewind rewind rewind rewind

20

46

Write each word or pair of letters eight times.
Try to keep them all the same size.

u u u u u u u u u

wall wall wall wall wall wall wall wall wall

oo oo oo oo oo oo oo oo oo

room room room room room room room room

ss ss ss ss ss ss ss ss ss

pass pass pass pass pass pass pass pass pass

tt tt tt tt tt tt tt tt

dotty dotty dotty dotty dotty dotty dotty dotty

rr rr rr rr rr rr rr rr

starry starry starry starry starry starry starry

Write the word **sitting** or **standing** for each person.

sitting
sitting
standing
sitting
sitting
sitting
sitting
standing
sitting
sitting

Write each word three times.

arrangement arrangement arrangement arrangement

carefully carefully carefully carefully

missing missing missing missing

fluttering fluttering fluttering fluttering

flooring flooring flooring flooring

26

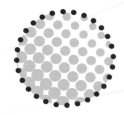

Copy the question mark as neatly as you
can, 15 times. Try to keep them all the same size.

? ? ? ? ? ? ? ? ? ? ? ? ? ? ? ?

? ? ? ? ? ? ? ? ? ? ? ? ? ? ?

? ? ? ? ? ? ? ? ? ? ? ? ?

Write each sentence carefully:

"Hello," said Tim.
"Goodbye," said Emily.
"Hello," said Tim.
"Goodbye," said Emily

"How are you?" asked Mr Patel.
"Very well, thank you," said Mrs Smith.
"How are you?" asked Mr Patel.
"Very well, thank you," said Mrs Smith.

"Do you know where my book is?"
asked Jasdeep.
"Where you left it, I expect," replied Kelda.
"Do you know where my book is?"
asked Jasdeep.
"Where you left it, I expect," replied Kelda.

32

47

Progress Check 6

Write the alphabet in capitals on the wavy line.

A B C D E F G H I J K L M N O P Q R S T U V W X Y Z

A B C D E F G H I J K L M N O P Q R S T U V W X Y Z

Write the alphabet in lower case letters on the wavy line. Look carefully at which letters join to the letters following them.

abcdefghijklmnopqrstuvwxyz

abcdefghijklmnopqrstuvwxyz

Copy the rhyme and then the cinquain poem really neatly.

This is the way
To do writing today.

This is the way
To do writing today.

My house
Is quite little.
There are two rooms downstairs,
Up the stairs there are just two more.
It's home.

My house
Is quite little.
There are two rooms downstairs,
Up the stairs there are just two more.
It's home.

38

Progress Check 7

Copy this conversation very neatly.

"What is the capital city of Australia?"
asked the teacher.
"I think it's Canberra," the pupil replied.

"What is the capital city of Australia?"
asked the teacher.
"I think it's Canberra," the pupil replied.

Use your best handwriting to copy the start of this short story.

Just as the clock struck midnight, Sam
sat up in bed. Now was his chance! He
slipped out of bed as quietly as he could
then tiptoed over to the door. The hinges
squeaked slightly as Sam pulled the door
open, but nobody else seemed to hear them.

Just as the clock struck midnight, Sam
sat up in bed. Now was his chance! He
slipped out of bed as quietly as he could
then tiptoed over to the door. The hinges
squeaked slightly as Sam pulled the door
open, but nobody else seemed to hear them.

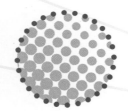

44